A SINNER SAYS

Sanjiv Bhatla was born in 1953. He graduated in electrical engineering from one of India's leading Institutes, and worked in that profession till 1985. Since then he has been mostly active as a freelance writer. His first book of poems, *Looking Back* was published in 1990, and the next, *Haiku, My Friend* in 1993. Bhatla was one of the founding members of The Society for Promotion of Poetry, and edited its quarterly journal, *Poetry Chronicle* between 1989 and 1993. His novel, *Injustice* was long-listed for the Man Asian Literary Prize, 2007.

By the same author
*

Looking Back
(Orient Longman Ltd.)
ISBN 0 86311 134 3

Haiku, My Friend
(Rupa & Co.)
ISBN 81 7167 153 5

A SINNER SAYS

(*Prompted by* The Dhammapada)

A Long Poem in Three Parts

By

SANJIV BHATLA

Crabwise Press™

First published in 2010
By Crabwise Press
Post Bag: 01, Nalasopara (West),
Thane 401203, Maharashtra, INDIA
Email: info@crabwisepress.in

ISBN 978-81-910777-0-4

CONDITION OF SALE

Acknowledgement

Acknowledgement is due to the editors of *Debonair* in which some sections of this poem first appeared.

The source of the article "Boy chosen by Dalai dumps monastery, turns to films", the text of which appears as the background in the cover design, is: *The Times of India.* © Bennett, Coleman & Co. Ltd. All rights reserved.

Acknowledgement is due to Orient Blackswan Ltd. for late Nissim Ezekiel's quote on the back cover.

Dedicated

To the memory of my parents

CONTENTS

FLESH

(I)

Grossly
One-sided, but
Engrossing game of Man
Versus God began long ago,
Bhikshu.

Unlike a bat, the Man had eyes: God's first
Deft move or design, *Bhikshu;*
The Cycle of the Day & Night, His next.
Man opened his eyes, and saw
Sometimes the light, then fathom upon a
Fathom of the dark beneath
A starry sky; he turned his head this way
And that, and saw nothing but
The dark; brought his gaze and thought back to where
His body was, and saw nothing but the dark --
Hour upon an hour he sat huddled
Thus, aware only of his breath
Going in and out, again in, and out;
Stopped his breath for a change
To know the result:
The Earliest Curiosity,
And knew in the resulting convulsion

13

The Earliest Fear.
Night upon a night the poor man sat
Thus, steeped in the Earliest Awareness
God, *Bhikshu*, had designed or deigned
The man to have: that he had an
Encapsulated breathing machine he
Could call his own, head to toe, prick rump and
Teeth, and everything else, everything beyond,
Was others, outside, not his.

The cyclical Day and, Sight were God's
First designs, *Bhikshu*. Haven't you ever
Seen a little dog, unintroduced, given
No time yet to find life's intricacies,
When left in the open at night trying
To sneak indoors? Throwing his head from side
To side, whimpering, wanting to go indoors,
Or wherever there's light?
Have you seen that little dog's eyes, *Bhikshu*?

That shocked and lost Neanderthal man was my father.

(II)

Born to a world of barren vast, lava, volcanoes –
The frightened, curious, baffled man. Lashed
On all sides by a harsh sun, surrounded on all sides
By shrieking birds, roaring beasts, vultures, reptiles;
Lashed sometime by rain and deluge, at times by dust
And storm; surrounded nightly by nightly fears;
Suspicious of all roving legs, all roving eyes;
Running away on prickly stones, thorns, to land's
Unsighted end, returning to the lost starting-rock;
Leaping up to get away from it all, pulled harshly
Back by earth's tight gravity; tired and shackled;
Everywhere to go,
Yet nowhere to hide;
Scared and baffled,
Lost in freedom;
Alone with his worried eyes,
With his panting machine was born into a harsh
World this poor ancestor of mine, *Bhikshu*.

(III)

It was a strange new world
Of ill-equipped men and
Bad tempered animals. All,
Without exception, all
Confounded by God's
Yet another design:
The primordial itch to
Eat, and not get eaten up.

Could God not make the sciences differently,
Bhikshu? Of course, He could. As perhaps He
Already has, on other stars and planets,
For all you and I know. For example,

He could make the man and
Beast not need to Eat, but Inhale
The nourishment needed
For sustenance in gaseous form
Directly from the air;
Not defecate, but pass
Out all waste in gaseous

16

Form through anus, mouth and nostrils
Directly back to the air;
And trees and plants, too, not need
The excreta as manure to survive and thrive,
But absorb the gaseous live-stock waste
Again directly from the air,
And return by osmosis,
Evaporation through bark, flower
Leaves, and other means oxygen,
Carbohydrates, vitamins, and proteins,
All in gaseous form
Directly to the air
For men and beast to merrily
Inhale nourishment all over
Again, and the cycle to continue,
So on and so forth, *ad infinitum*,
Ad nauseam, you see, *Bhikshu*?

No Food, no Fight!

You and I have
Seen aliens from
Other planets;

17

But have you, or
I seen them eat?
No, no?

The Pump, the wonderful pump would
Then acquire the composite job
Of purifying, producing, and pushing blood
In a mad rush through each Machine;
Each Machine would then depend
Only on dear father God's free
Pool of air, and not depend on any animal's,
Or any other beastly man's machine, you see!

But that was not to be.
Not these, but a different
Set of three P's God had
On His mind; three loaded dice
That the Father at once
Threw at the baffled child
And put him on the mat
For all intent, purpose, and times.

(IV)

The fear to not get eaten up gave man
Tact. The God-made recurring Hunger made
Man want to Possess, then possess some more,
And hide himself and his prey from others'
Roving, hungry eyes – the first hints
Of Guile.

God wished all men to Plan to Possess
All the time, *Bhikshu*. Each by himself; each
Darting shouts and spears, arrows and nasty
Stares at the other, with
Not a word of Language
Between them to assuage
Mutual fears, to bridge the stinking
Brooks of mistrust surging between
Them, to shield the dirty glances
Shooting all around;

No shake of hands
Was introduced yet; no
Touching of cheeks

19

Yet premised; not a
Hint on the interpretation
Of the broadest smile –

God only wanted to see the man
Fight, and fight more –
Bounce up and down, run away,
Crouch, stare, in real or trivial fears,
Stay within his confines – but never,
Never, to jump across the stinking brooks . . .
To reach out to his fellow homosapiens.

The Father's idea of a joke!

Language did evolve, *Bhikshu*, over the time, but
Much after God's designs had firmly taken root
In man's body, soul, and mind.

(V)

Pain inflicted by prickly pebbles and stone spears
Made man love the touch of smooth round boulders. That he
Actually bent down and kissed them, I can not say, but
Surely loved to caress them in marvel:
A gradual honing of the hassled man's
Desire for the woman's round Breast.
"Milk-provision for the kids", did you say,
Bhikshu? No, no way. That was not on God's mind. Else,
He could make the breast penis-like,
Like a cow's teats, more convenient
To suckle, surely?
Udders, why have not one, but one plus one
Two udders placed prominently
On woman's chest, and her teats,
So small relatively, even
Unreachable sometimes, convoluted
Inside, if milk-provision was the main
Purpose on God's mind?
And why round? Why not
Horizontal Egyptian pyramid-like?
He could have easily

Stuck a bone here, and stuck a bone there,
If you see what I mean?

God made the breasts round, just the right
Size to fill man's two palms. Besides,
Unlike guava, pear, plum, pumpkin,
Orange melon or peach, sweetly
Squeezable to both the parties utter
Delight; just the right enticement
For the pain-hating souls.
     See the Woman,

Bhikshu, deftly slipping between the folds.
And here the plot thickens with the glue.

(VI)

God, *Bhikshu*, had no favorites.
His four-legged animals
And the two-legged ones
All lived aloof, yet all

Watchful of their fellow
Men and fellow beasts, each
Looking askance at their smaller
Leg between legs that secreted glue.

The four-legged ones forgot killing
When it stood up;
The two-legged ones forgot killing
When it stood up;
Man stood up,
Clutched
The muscle rod hard, pumped it hard,
His smithy machine hurling breath into nostrils
Like thin paper ruffle reruffle in wind --
Shut his eyes in sun
And
   Exploded
        Sky.

Eh, *Bhikshu*! The Earliest, Great Discovery!
What do you say?

(VII)

Get this straight, *Bhikshu*,
Once and for all:
I did not make the Woman.

For that matter, I did not make
Her thighs chunky and soft, and the
Juice rinse up between them in pink
And dark pink tender folds of flesh...
And she wanting hard the muscle rod shoved hard
Into the pouting flesh, and the man wanting
Hard to shove harder and splutter his and her juice, both
Wanting the act that was both violence and joy at once:

A new feeling
Of intensity
That was different from
The intensity
Of Fear or Rancour. Discovery
Of passion with a capital p,
That was to glue the society.

Well: interesting situation.
Man the two-and-a-half legged was watchful
Of animals, and other two-and-a-half
Legged ones, but here was a half-a-leg-short!
And instead with a lovely hole there, to boot!
Looking a little different,
A Little less strong --
All on God's design.
Man for the first time shared his fears
With the juice; for the first time sensed
A welcome diversion
From fearing alone, fearing aloneness; sensed
The Will to Protect someone other than himself:
Felt the first shades of Love.

But alas, he sensed also a renewed
Reminder of the dark, of loneliness,
After the burst;
Felt emptiness of a different kind,
The possible genesis of the word
Indifference – of a different kind,
After the burst.
The man sensed a suspicion

Of a different kind this time around:
Born out of a will to protect
Not food, not self, but someone of his own kind,
Felt perhaps for the first time,
A sense of Collective Self,
Togetherness; possibly the genesis of the word
Humankind -- post the coital burst.

(VIII)

"What burst? What juice? Your talk is disgusting. Rubbish."
"Ram Ram Ram
Hari Hari"
"God made Woman simply to make
Children, to perpetuate the freshness of mornings;
That is why He made Day and Night,
Night to rest and sleep peacefully ..."

Shut up, *Bhikshu*. And pay attention.

(IX)

Three P's ploughed the man's barren
Mind: to Plan, Possess, and Protect.
The little ones came and man
Made the Home, the Word, the Commune –
Desirous to share with his fellow men
The weakness born out of the fear
To protect alone; to ward
Off his fellow men's desire for
His woman, his food, and other things
In his store.

The passion-sodden man looked
Around, snarled with mistrust --
This Killer and Protector --
And produced, when the muscle
Rod had cooled,
A different sort of glue:
Norms to instill a different kind

Of fear in his fellow men's minds:
A whole lot of

Codes of Conduct for the whole commune.

To Plan, Possess, and Protect the man found welcome
Diversions from feeling, and fearing Aloneness.
This indulgence, together with
The never-leaving,
Always-tailing ever since
The first dark night,
The same old
Feeling of Aloneness,
Shaped man's sense of Identity:
Evolution of his Ego.

Hunger, fear and woman made man want to
Plan, possess and protect; woman, fear,
And hunger made man plough his barren mind;
To protect, possess, and the Aloneness
Gave the Planner his ego; ego
And Aloneness made man want
To plan, protect, and possess
More:
The first shades of Hope.

Ego, fear and the Mind made
Man form the commune;
Create the Language --
To assuage fear, aid purpose,
To understand, not misunderstand --
To aid the man create
A whole lot of norms
Of Conduct and Censure,
Morals and Religion:
For the whole commune.

Understood, *Bhikshu*?!

(X)

Morals and Religion:
Woman gave Man morals and religion.

The instinct for survival, instilled
Deeper than fear, in pain, beyond
Fear of eradication;
The recurring hunger of stomach,
Groin, and greed, the cause of hope, beyond
Hope of eradication;
The constant suspicion of the Other,
Known much before the Language, beyond
Eradication by word spoken, or told.

Man knew victory, and man knew defeat,
In the discovery of woman's
Inequality man knew dubious
Defeat and dubious Victory.
The play of ego
And the play of love
Made a heady concoction:
A gradual emergence of the word
Human, and the phrase, Human Frailty.

Sex was declared a sin.
Clothes were created, many
Many layers of them;

Freedom was creating
Problems: rules of conformity,
Rituals, lines to tow were
Created, their virtues extolled;
Hoodoo, magic, ghosts and witches
Were invented to decry those
Found greedy of groin's saliva;
Shame and Guilt were created;
Hurting anyone with a spear,
Word or act was named Bad,
And a U.P.A.:
Universal Punishing Authority,
    The Good God
Was created by man many
Many years ago --
Soon after the creation of communes.

Woman is the Mother of the Good God.

The mother of man
In desperate combat
Against the designs of the real, evil God.

31

(XI)

Let us not mistake   this, *Bhikshu*:
There are two Gods: *The* God,
And Man's God.
Man's God   is but a myth, merely
A reaction   to *The* God's sadistic
Actions and designs.
So, naturally, he's benign!

Why do you think Newton's Law
Of Action & Reaction holds true
Universally, *Bhikshu*?
Because it's *The* God's will.
What would otherwise its sanctity be?
Why should there be in this world
A reaction in the first place, and why
Not half, or double, or one fifth --
Why always equal to the action, and
Opposite, to boot?
Because the real God has willed it thus.
No arguments, *Bhikshu*!

It was *The* God's will to make man
Create an illusion and bang
His head against it; it was His
Will to haunt the man with perpetual
Miseries of the real or imagined
Kind, fears real or imagined, doubts valid
Or doubtful, efforts belied or fructified.

The man was destined to be dissatisfied,
Even in gain –
Always running from one to another
Mirage; unhappy with every solace,
Finding the newer solace tepid,
Searching for yet another
Of real or imagined kind!

Dark humor of that Sadist!

What self-flagellation,
My poor man!
Groping, evolving, such terms
As a Kind God; seeking mercy
In this birth; seeking to atone

In rebirth; donning up guilt
That wasn't your own in the first place;
Seeking to purify your soul
When the dirt wasn't your own;
Chastising yourself for sins
That weren't your own in the first place –
Always seeking pardon,
For fuck alone knows what!
Always seeking to merge your soul
With that God whose only goal was to deny you peace!

Such defeat!

(XII)

And that defines my religion, *Bhikshu*.
I say -- screw the business of the two Gods,
To begin with --
And care for your fellow-suffering
Homosapiens; understand
One another; give a good shot
To not misunderstand
One another, poor souls
Huddle together, you, and love,
Just care for one another
Homo sapiens!
Forlorn children!
It's a dark, dark sky...
And there's no God who loves you.

(*End of the First Part*)

MIND

Passion found diversions. Barred now
From hiding in a hole like an ostrich, subjugated
More to the Law of Alone -- or Identity,
Passion, with ego and mind formed the society.

Village, town and city.
Mortar, mud, cow-dung,
Clay-bricks, logs and hay;
Roads to connect, junctions
For a choice or diversion.
Decorations for the house;
Fire for a sermon, for a glow;
Lamps and the lights
To shoo away the night.

Barter system
For the goods. Woman's
Body recently sheathed,
Available for a price:
The Oldest Profession.
Wheat, maize, or millet.

Water churning machine, methods to irrigate;
Steam for the kettle-lid, engines, turbines;
Using friction to make the cart wheel roll,
The windmill rotate: hope-propelled ingenuity ...
And behind it, a happy, eager mind.

Village, town and city, and a society
For each: each made
Porous by the man-made word.
Man formed, and farmed them
Through ego, passion and mind.

(II)

Hardly had the man decorated
The paper lamp-shades with sketches
Of a crowned head, flowers and butterflies,
Hanging from the rafters, swaying in the
Breeze to the lilt of a song and
A pluck of the strings --
Hardly had the man started

Loving the new way of Being
  That he heard
In the deeper depths of the night
Death's footsteps.
A feeble yet persistent
Knocking on his mind's door.
Hardly had the poor man overcome
The fear of the spear and the sword
That he now felt weakened by the new
Fear of eventual, inevitable, and complete
Cessation of his lovely life: by Death.

Mankind's mind
Has grown cumulatively
With time;
Man's own little mind
Dies with his death. His ego,
Love, newly learnt laughter, newly
Enjoyed comfort, emotions newly
Discovered, all perish
With death.

Death destroys man's ego
And passion, so the two in reaction
Derive strength from its awareness
Through the mind.
Death plays on a man's mind,
Because his ego and passion
Play only until death.

Voices of the gods and the wise men fallen quiet
As the centuries rolled, banishing all oracles, ceasing
All celestial help to the thought-weaver, society-maker,
All hints on how to go further about, leaving him
More and more alone with his weak jelly mind --
Aware only that Death would scythe him one day.
Having drawn the poor man sufficiently
Into the habit of Desiring:
Desiring to understand, desiring
To improve; desirous of peace,
Desirous to be in control --
Making the man believe he had earned a right
To desire more,
Your God, *Bhikshu*,
Let go of his little finger, saying, go, go sucker,

Now you are on your own!

How could the smart man sit quiet!

Predictably, per force of what was now a habit
Of reacting to God's designs, confident
Of owning a thinking mind, having
Seen the confident mind's other
Satisfactory produce: morals, religion,
Well-oiled, fully-functional society machine,
Demurely smiling maidens flitting about,
Their shame decently wrapped in clean clothes;
Man, this time around, showing
He was still in full control,
That there was nothing
Beyond his understanding,
Took on Death, pompously,
And invented, to lessen its agony,
A non-existent heaven:

Nirvana!

Another myth, like the good-god,
To bang his head against,
Another hallowed mirage to chase,
Another desperate bid
Of the caged man to paint his cage sky-blue.

(III)

You refuse to understand *Bhikshu*, that's what bugs me.
You brag on about your own self-righteous stuff,
While here I am, taking so much pain, talking sense to you!
There is no such thing as Truth, as preached by you;
Your Truth, in fact, is miles away from the real God' will;
There is no such thing as Harmony with the Self,
As preached by you.

You define harmony with the self
In a Rigid manner, not Relative.
You see wisdom in denial, or suppression
Of the ego, and not in its acceptance as it is.
To me, it is a defeatist acceptance

Of Self's limitations in regard to ego's reach –
Because the Self can not match up to ego's dreams,
Let's kill the ego, or suppress it,
Batter it beyond recognition,
Make a zombie out of every living being. Right?
To me, it is a reactionary ploy
Of your own ego who preaches this,
Or a cunning ploy of your ego to mitigate
The feeling of Aloneness differently
By merely being different!

If I say I'm in harmony with my self,
Content, at peace with my humble living,
Eating, sleeping, washing my clothes
With my own hands, letting the maid take a holiday;
Desireless -- as I pass by the bazaar
Slowly treading a footpath, wrapped-in, convinced;
Then I am, in fact, in harmony
With my Environment:
With my Self not in isolation,
But as embedded in the hodgepodge
Of my mind, and my world around.
For every different self embedded

In the hodgepodge of a different mind
And a different world, there's a different
Definition of harmony, according to me.
It's a kaleidoscope of the self,
Mind, and the world around;
Each little turn,
Each different combination
Of the three,
Creates a different
Picture of Harmony.

And that harmony would be real,
If I accept it as such.

For then it would mean I am in harmony
With my ego: both the slave and the master
Of the mind, which also determines
Self-harmony, or otherwise.
Environment desired, and that
Decreed by circumstance, present and past, are the only
True realities, as differentiated by ego and the mind
Present and past, affected and or inherited.

Grant to each man his own
Definition of harmony
That would grant him
Lasting peace, *Bhikshu*.
In the acceptance of my ego
Is my liberation,
Or its hope;
In the vehement denial
Of my ego, in its suppression,
In some elusive search
For some illusive *Nirvana* --
A new ostrich-syndrome --
My hopeless defeat.

(IV)

To search for *Nirvana* against the real God's will
As manifest in His 'gifts' to man, namely, hunger,
Passion and ego, pleasures of the tongue and the groin,
Looming presence of the mind, death and the fear
Of the dark, would be, according to me, getting

47

Into a no-win tug-of-war with Him.
Or, more appropriately, entering the pitch
For a rugby match and insisting to play soccer! Ha!
I could, if God has given me Compassion, at best
Call it an elitist pastime of the allegedly
Enlightened few like you.

Imagine, *Bhikshu*, this situation: let's say
The world were transformed all of a sudden,
As if by magic, into a world
With all sins halved, all desires reduced
By half. Then would you say that the entire
Mankind was half-way closer to *Nirvana*, or to God?

Imagine further: if you had the world
Completely, and suddenly, cleansed
Of all sins, all desires --
Everyone going around with stares fixed
Straight on, or heads bent down with furrowed
Brows, or permanent smiles pasted on their faces
Like morons; everyone living and eating
With full simplicity; sleeping, behaving with full
Chastity – having abdicated, renounced

48

All, and all memories
Of having lived differently
Erased from each mind, all standards
To compare erased:
Then would you say that the entire world
Had fully achieved *Nirvana*?

No, *Bhikshu*!
You wouldn't even notice the difference!

It would be a dull-dog world, for sure.
Some honest man would then
Come around using a simple prefix,
"My":
'My boring world',
To begin with;
'My bicycle'; 'my helicopter'.
He would then go around
Swaggering, rollicking,
Quenching the moons burning
Over the maidens' eyelids;
    Lavishing tributes
To the real God's will;

And lo!
You would then have a brand new definition,
Of what else . . . but *Nirvana*!

(V)

See that fisherman, *Bhikshu*?

The sun rises in Daman
As anywhere else, smearing
The leaves and the sails
With a dash of the yoke.
He will rise before the sun.
Shit and wash in the open, then
He will pass the thin strands of nylon-wire
Through small holes in a vertical stone-slab,
And entwine them.
Thus, he will have
A thicker cord.
He will pass the thicker cords through bigger holes
In the vertical stone-slab, and go on entwining them,

To make a still thicker,
Still stronger rope...
And so on, and so forth.

Then, he will sail far out on the sea, stop
Where there's only
Sun
Birds
And him:
He will cast his net.

Then he will sit,
Wait for the fish
Absently.
He will watch the plastic
Balls bob on the water,
Listen to the small
Waves break
Against his boat,
Absently.

He will come back and mount his woman for whom
And their children, he earns...

Then, he will sleep, as they say, like a log;
Fully at peace with his environment,
Oblivious of your exotic H with the S bit;
Fully in harmony with his ego, his self.

(VI)

To have an ability to plan, possess and protect,
And an awareness of it; and an awareness that it is
Not vastly different from another man's capabilities,
Is the perpetuation of every man's misery
As willed by the real God.

Empty tins, rags, and coconut shells: all
Ride the crest of a wave, almost in a line,
None too far ahead, or too far behind. Man's
Mind and physical capabilities
Have grown only thus.

Why do all men shoot the goal kick only a little
Beyond the centre line, or there about,

And not some straight into the opposite goalie's arms?
Why not some men take milliseconds, and not seconds,
Like all others, to dodge the ball?
Why do all men from Africa, Italy, Honolulu and Honduras,
Siberia and Nagapattanam, run the hundred yards
In ten seconds, or there about, and not some in six,
Or seven and a half?
Equality?

Yes. But not for Equanimity.
Equality, to increase Entropy
Among the human minds.

Those unable in the fierce combat
To win to possess more,
And then some more to benumb
The pain of combat, sulk.
They even hang themselves. Or kill.
Or seek *Nirvana*,
To live dead-like,
To hurry the death.

Bhikshu, have you heard of a Brahmin
Who had a hard-on while bathing in the Ganges
When he saw a woman's naked breasts?
You know what he did, *Bhikshu*?

He came out and shoved a nail into his penis.
Oops!

Such an ego, such anger at not being in control!
Such hope!

(VII)

"Compassion to him too, he who succumbs",
I know you will say. Well, ego's ways...

"Don't, don't put words into my mouth, you rascal,
Loafer; don't cook up stories to humiliate
Good men in search of truth; you insult your
Creator; you ignorant fool! May He forgive you. You ..."

Keep quiet, *Bhikshu*.
And just listen to me.

Well, I was telling you, the ego's ways
Are many: some more obvious,
Like inflicting pain to others,
Or scoring victories over others;
Some, deceptively shrouded,
Like causing pain to the self,
Or self-flagellation,
Through Compassion.

Those disbursing compassion
Unconditionally, left right and centre,
Are quack saints who
Make a living out of
Looking compassionate.
True saints too are
Omni-compassionate,
But they have channeled
Their ego into the self-flagellation way.
There too are the truly compassionate
Among the ordinary ones like me, but they look

Down upon the ones they
Are being compassionate to.
Right, *Bhikshu*? Again

A kind of victory,
Or self-flagellation of another kind.

Those with satiated ego and passion
Are more honest like a child:
Less compassionate. Or, only
Selectively so:
Not omni-so.

When I was a child, *Bhikshu*, I wouldn't spare
Even the earth, let alone the boy who stole my marbles.
When I fell down running, for example,
I wouldn't stop crying until my mother
Spanked the ground with her slippers a few times, chanting,
"Beat you, beat you, you naughty earth, you bad earth,
You hurt my little boy!"
Then I would feel better, 'beat' the earth
A few times myself, and run along.
(To settle it with the boy who I thought stole my marbles.)

Peel the layers off a man until you see
The child. The layers of greed, guile,
Acquired as the process of growing up,
Becoming 'mature'. The layers of environment
Of his own, and of others, living and dead;
Environment real, or simulated, acquired,
And or inherited through ego, passion,
And mind of his own, and or those of others
Around, in keeping up with the Joneses,
Present and past. The beautiful
Child unrecognizable under the multiple layers
Of it all – deceit, conceit, desire, acerbity
And what not – unrecognizable as an adult.

Compassion, for such a man, *Bhikshu*,
Is merely an indulgence:
Showing fake concern for others:
A way of turning his mind away
From his passion and ego;
A way of burning his unspent
Passion and ego – determined
Unspent by his mind,
In the face of his worldly limitations,

In the wake of an awareness of death.

That is how I have known it, *Bhikshu*,
That is how I have enjoyed it, suffered it.
I have seen things from others' perspective,
Given them leeway for all their behaviors,
All their shenanigans,
Given them the benefit of the doubt
Even for such things as they themselves
Do not consciously realize, out of compassion,
And they have always made me
Feel happy, by making me sad!
They have helped me burn
My unspent hash!

I have known it thus, *Bhikshu*.
One may call it the right way
Of progressively achieving disinterest,
Progressively achieving *Nirvana*;
I have known it as progressively
Achieving death -- the right way.

(End of the Second Part)

I

(I)

Bhikshu, I know the truth.

It was God's own will, evil,
To give the man all that that He did --
Like a mischievous brat going
To a zoo, and putting a thorny
Crown over a monkey's head!
It was God's will, too, to make
The 'monkey' like the hat; get bruised,
Yet feel happy with the hat;
Unhappy at times, but always
Possessive of it; love it, clutch
It to the bosom – then smash it
Hard against the ground, jump on it,
Proclaim to have renounced it,
Then pick it up again with a grin!
Fed up of, yet unable to
Live without the hat;
Gripping it, yet gripped

Himself tightly by the hat, the pathetic man, *Bhikshu*!

61

Not knowing why he wants to possess, why
Protect; his flesh garnished with the sediments
Of his father's flesh, his blood infused
With the blood of many forefathers
Well into the past,
To the pure blood
Infused with the real God's evil designs.

The pathetic man adorning himself
With responsibilities for a mere
Want of them, not knowing that the want
Itself did not origin with his own breath;
Struggling, giving or finding reasons,
Coining terms like Sin or Salvation;
Calling being true as getting away
From the truth, calling untruthful
The path of the truth;
Seeking light, shunning the lights,
Not knowing the impregnable,
Primordial dark in his soul.

Lonely depths of the dark sky stretch out
Far within this forlorn man's heart,

Left alone to burn his, and in his,
Ego and passion until death.
Gravity stills tires him, pins him down,
Though marking boulders are now given street names;
Scorching sun still abounds, though prickly rocks
Have been rounded off in beds and one-night stands;
The fear of the Other still remains, though
It has spilled out from the man's cave
Into every nook and corner of the concrete
World; the brooks of suspicion still turn
Among men, despite suave language
And all other ways to communicate:
In moving elevators
It colors the unseen shade on every face.
The search for Freedom still remains,
Though it has traversed many a mile
To holiday-homes, monasteries, and hill-resorts.
The world, *Bhikshu*,
Hasn't really changed!
A perfect enacting to the finest last detail
Of your Evil God's design:
Faithful, oh my god, how horridly faithful to it
Even over a million years' time!

Everyday, I see those God-fearing men
Traveling in local trains,
Half asleep, eyes half closed
In a daze, nostrils whiffling
Gentle snores –- or, idly
Looking out,
Hands in lap;

I look at them intently,
Bhikshu: I can almost see
An innocent child in every face!
Or, a few others, standing, holding
The handle bars above their heads
Look to me like dressed up apes!
All quiet, all having something on their minds....

Isn't there something fundamentally
Morbid here, *Bhikshu*?

I love this man; I call this love
The terminal hope for us homosapiens;
And in the knowledge of the Real Design
     I sin

Against both Gods.
I react, and oscillate between the two,
Touch neither, I recede from both.
I cling to the derelict man, his slow death,
I sing the hapless ode to both...
And thus I sin not,
As per my book, *Bhikshu*!

(II)

Carrying the burden of the Neanderthal Man,
I, at a loss,
Ruing and raving alike
The passing lights.

Now, chugging along like a lone shunting engine
Amidst the hum of corona discharge
Between tall voltage wires, amidst
Weeds, I feel strangely full of joy,
Unnaturally reassured in continuities
That exist only in the mind, present and past;

Hearing the crinky-crank of a bicycle wheeled
Slowly, in days when not riding was a possible choice,
I see the busy traffic of my city with disdain,
"Above it," as if.
The sun sets now above the tall buildings
Just as it set above the gravel path then,
And in this continuity of the gray sky,
From here, to there,
From now, into the past,
I have felt the warmth of smoke-laden evenings
Extinct, but flushed close to me even now....

These continuities, out of a wish to protect,
Cling to, even that which is now really no more,
Are the stuff our memories are made of, *Bhikshu*.
Soothing, because reminiscence is a possession,
And therefore, a way of dissipation of the ego.

But that was not how the home was, *Bhikshu*.
Always an abstract concept, ever in transition;
The wish to continually possess and protect more
And more always made the home peaceless,
A mere corollary, never a cherished goal,

So never realized, always disfigured,
Discolored in a flux of passion and ego,
Seen in totality only in reminiscing,
Longed for when gone,
Never loved....

I, now alone, therefore
More free to stare
The ego in the face,
Have grown quietly
Like the plant growing in my balcony
All day, in the sun, all by itself....
These tender affinities
Shrieking at the switch of a lamp
When I return home nightly,
Have made me grow
Through decay. I have seen
The futility of growth and decay alike:
The futility of the joy of growth,
The futility of the fear of decay:
Both the silly ploys of death,
This way, or that.

I have seen the tips of tall corn glistening
In the setting sun like a fieldful of glow-worms
Summoned at noon;
I have spent time seeing the constant
Flicker and dance of the bright dots
Spread as far and wide as eye could see,
A shimmering restlessness
Spread as far and wide as vision could go,
A crescendo of the powers of God;
I have wondered if all Art
Wasn't but the freakish joy
Of the Neanderthal Man's son,
A silly exercise at matching the wits with God,
An exercise at catharsis; and all Science:
Knowledge assembled, amassed over the ages
Through a continuity of Mind,
But a silly attempt to understand God's will,
To systematize the compulsion to stay alive!

What have they given us, *Bhikshu*!

I now crave for a world of make-beliefs.
Of sun and the shade, hammock and the tall

Glasses of lemonade; of bizarre schemes
Of mischief; love, no lechery, lilt
And innocence; pigs, thieves on the
Bicycle, solitary policemen; goodness
Made real beyond belief;
Of moons and the lakes,
Maidens, lazy dogs;
Of sweetness and milky
Laughter, leisure -- beyond all pain:
My fairyland of characters as old as I am now,
Yet as young as I was,

Playing the chequer-game
With my father every evening. Cheating!

Evenings now grow colossal, *Bhikshu*.

Walking through the twilight glow
Of late-night neons,

On empty roads, when
Even the vehicles move

With a lazy drone, half asleep,
I have heard the clock tick-tock

Very noisily.

I have felt the spherical
Symmetry of the universe.

And in it trapped my soul.

In my youth I used to
Play with rugby balls, my eyes,

Knock them on and catch them back
From every wall of busy stores,

And walk out with purposeful steps,
Not really knowing where to go.

There is no recourse,
No escape,

Even to be indifferent
Is to implicate,
To be free is to
Be shackled
In one way or another.

I walk on, having everywhere and nowhere to go!
Nowhere to go, nowhere to hide!

Two rogues share the booty
Down a long, Sunday corridor.
It's mockery, all the way.

The End

The End